FUCKING ANIMALS

"It is refreshing to read the sexual adventures of a college boy who is gay . . . . sets whole sexual romantic, nature-sympathetic overtones going."
—Jim Eggeling, *The Advocate*

"In Arabic poetry, the male moon is adolescent . . . . But the moon is best known as a fecundating repository of light. . . . Edmund Miller writes of his lover, 'he retracts / the foreskin of the stormy sky— / I see the moon.'"
—Gregory Woods, *Articulate Flesh: Male Homoeroticism and Modern Poetry*

"Amid the oak, hard as a cock . . . / sliver / Of the gods' desire, . . . Edmund Miller . . . asks for nuts / For tits and tots. . . ."
—John J. Soldo, author of *Sonnets for Our Risorgimento*

"Edmund Miller should be praised for the honesty of blending a scholarly career with a vocation of whimsical creativity. His poems say what gay men feel but few write about, and he expresses himself with a verve and elegance never far from erudition and rarely far from eroticism."
—George Klawitter, editor of *The Complete Poems of Richard Barnfield*

"Edmund Miller's *Fucking Animals* has acquired a kind of legendary status as an underground publication. The poems are witty, playful, and sometimes outrageous. It is good to see them back in print."
—Claude J. Summers, editor of *Gay and Lesbian Literary Heritage*

"Edmund Miller's poetry is gaily lyrical yet compact and intense; it rejoices in life's little details while evoking another world of artifice and ecstasy. And the Afterword raises literary criticism to a new dimension of playful self-reflection."
—Charles M. Kovich, author of *First Things First*

"If you're gay and big meat turns you on, try *Fucking Animals* you'll be a vegetarian the rest of your life."
—Michael Perkins, *Screw*

FUCKING ANIMALS: A BOOK OF POEMS
REVISED EDITION WITH NEW AFTERWORD

BY EDMUND MILLER

Florida Literary Foundation Press
Sarasota
1994

Previous publication:
The poems on the pages indicated were previously published: 5 *Haiku Spotlight*, 15 *Escutcheon*, 19 *Tangents*, 21 *Hey Lady!*, 27 *Haiku Highlights*, 4, 21, 36, 45, 53, and 58 *Mouth of the Dragon*, 60 and 61 *Concepts*

By the same author:
Leavings Northport: Birnham Wood Graphics, 1995.
The Happiness Cure; and, Other Poems Northport: Birnham Wood Graphics, 1993.
George Herbert's Kinships: An Ahnentafel with Annotations Bowie MD: Heritage P, 1992.
Editor with Robert DiYanni. *Like Season'd Timber: New Essays on George Herbert* New York: Peter Lang, 1987.
A Rider of Currents Lakewood OH: Quality Publications, 1986.
Editor. *Mount-Orgueil: or Divine and Profitable Meditations* by William Prynne: A Facsimile Edition Delmar: Scholars' Facsimiles & Reprints, 1984.
Exercises in Style 1980; New York: privately printed, 1990.
Drudgerie Divine: The Rhetoric of God and Man in George Herbert Salzburg: Universität Salzburg, 1979.
Winter New York: Randall International, 1975.
The Nadine Poems New York: Randall International, 1973.
The School for Coeds New York: privately printed, 1972.

Disclaimer: Throughout this poetry, the word "boy" denotes a college student over eighteen years of age. The word "child" is a meiosis: the child is the father of the man. And no suggestion is made that persons under the age of eighteen ever engage in sex, think about sex, or serve as the objects of erotic fantasy.

ISBN 1-877978-70-1
Library of Congress Catalogue No. 94-068045
© 1973; new material © 1994 Edmund Miller

Contents

Parking	1
Women	2
Seen	3
Edwardian Insight	4
Hokku	5
Donnée	6
Old Jersey	7
Hokku	8
Eyeful	9
The Glass Ass	10
Most Valuable Rookie	11
Pæderastia	12
It Off	14
Near-Occasional Poem	15
Hokku	16
Hokku	17
On B. R. 1	19
Roadside Stand	20
Boy	21
A Man	22
Senryu	24
Oh, to Keep Beauty Back	25
Barstop	26
Straight	27
Hokku	28
Paul Call	29
Some Children	30
Some Children	31
Epistle to the Mod Church	32
Passing	33
Track Meat	34
Hokku	36
Senryu	37
Old Jersey	38
Fraternity	40

Fraternity	41
Below the Belt	42
Another Anniversary	43
Hokku	44
Senryu	45
Catch	46
No Accident	47
Seen	48
Seen	49
Play by Ear	50
A Phi Delt in Charbert's	51
Hokku	52
Hokku	53
Two Sides	54
Accumulated Interest	55
Hokku	56
Hokku	57
Incident	58
Incident	59
Hokku	60
Hokku	61
Sucking Up	62
Quickie	63
Seen	64
The Daydream	65
Senryu	66

*

Index of Forms	67
Allusion Index	68
A More Sporting Index	69
Words Not Known to the WordPerfect™ Spellcheck	70
Afterword	73
About the Author	84

♂♂

*For the Ohio State football team ('69),
who made it all possible.*

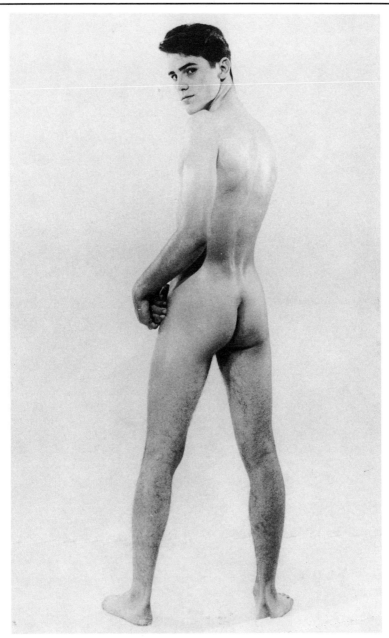

Bill Rice photographed by Troy Saxon

PARKING

The park is so full of young lovers
That the couples bump into each other
As they look about
For places
To dream.

WOMEN

Trojans shore up the defenses,
Dull the senses.
Greasy Helen baits the hook.
And Troy is took.

SEEN

You make your whole jaw move while you chew—
And your cheekbones too.
And still your mouth is closed,
And you talk in nods.
And she lets you—that way—
Do all the talking
And, so, gets you that way.

EDWARDIAN INSIGHT

Decadence is setting in.
A gilded hunk is sitting in
This library across from me,
His crotch accosting me.
Shorted in a tight, off-white get-up,
The hunk won't let it up or get it up.
But its shape is well-defined enough
To say he wants me not to get enough.
And, of necessity, its visible anatomy
Begins to stir the man in me.

HOKKU

Flowers on my shirt
Grow at night, then fade away . . .
Artificial day.

DONNÉE

Agreed, you are pretty, great,
Sweet piece, Gregory the Eight.
I am only your every over-leg-looker.
But I am not la crosse you bear. Hook y'r
Stick up, Greg. Keep your
Both hands on stick. Ignore
Me. For some are the doers;

I may try your un-Donne to be.
You may see no health in me;
In us no fun may plea.
Ah, but you play my game with me
Just now when you think you see
Always looking straight at you me.

OLD JERSEY

Here we have a lineman
Sitting in the library
In the beautifully deceptive utility
Of his shy underjersey.
Mostly he wears it
Because it's roomy.
And its issue is after all official for
A lockerroom swell.
And it clings so well,
Shaping without telling
The exact extent of the swelling
And of the welling of his inevitable curves.
And this coffee cake and sugared sticky mass
With none, alas, of the glossy new ass or jack
Of your typical glamorous passing back,
None of those cocky moves all over the place,
Just the unassuming raw lumber of the line,
Wears his jersey, see, especially
Because it's so very warmly
Womby.

HOKKU

The wind in the tree—
An æolian harping
On thee.

EYEFUL

    My strangeness (pre-arranged, this) catches, cuts your eye. Aware,
You take an enormous headfilling eyeful in in
Your enormous, frazzle-fragile headsize eyes.
The electric, neon christmas tree you see in me amazes, dazzle-dazes.
Your tightening, piercing momentary takeback asks'm I for real. Yeah.
Your swearing glaring, your cloze-up in close-up,
Your eyelining eyelash slapdash flicker-flash,
Your beautifully bloodshot reflex stare,

    Reflects. I see you too.
You don't frighten me: you enlighten me, lighten me.
The beauty I see reels me. You happen, and I'm happied into reverie.
I breathe your breathing-down-my-neck all-round-me-ness as caress.
You see—I carry all my life about with me.
Now you live with me. You become my poetry.

THE GLASS ASS

He comes toward me in the glassdoor mirroring
Because I am not looking where.
He walks through into the realitynight outdoors
On the other side,
Bringing his beautifully broken arm
With him through life,
Shifting it from left to right,
Shifting his weight from sinister to straight
With his waist dipping back,
His hips moving on.

MOST VALUABLE ROOKIE

The goal, their orient,
Is your goal,
Goalie Chris.
Tonguing the mask
Masking your tonguing,
Melting the rink
And the bleachers,
Your hot mouth huge
With rinky-think encouragements,
You're happy home on ice.
And you stick to your goal,
Give icemen their due,
Let each take out on you
His nice violence,
His stick-whipping,
His man-thing.

PÆDERASTIA:
THE PROGRESS OF A LUMINARY LUCIFER
GROWING UP BETWEEN THE WARS

While some Bill S. Heartthrob drags anagrammatic araB deaTH
Across the screens,
Callipygian catamites cavort through the Twentyish mind—
"Oh, the religious innocence of children in church!
Boychicks of my dreaming,
Toy tricks of my scheming,
Coy flicks of my screaming,
I'm only a child at hard;
Protect me from yourselves."
Yet out of the mouths of those polymorphous perverse
What seems may come:

Phosphorescent days dissolve into florescent nighthood
As sybarites sodomize with earnest quadriviality.
Here and there: "No unescorted males admitted."
But there is never nearly enough No.
The gay signs flick on and off
Disclosing cute couplings in anonymous and temporary motels.
A boy with Madras eyeshadow breaks wrist and wind for a year or a week
Breeding only infectious friends.
Then, for an hour, George à Greene plays Primrose Pricker of Wakefield.
But "There was much Z,"
Reports K. Kafka Tchaikovsky.

After the noon of the night,
When the wanderlusting's through,
The sperm-scented sheets of youth
("Joy kicks of my reaming")

Are superseded in a sanguine coup
And held in check through fear—
With love and psychiatry,
Tender, caring psychiatry.
The venereal suburbs seep into the groin,
And they are always hungrily celibate thereafter,
Drinking.

And that's quite another skylark
From quite another spring.

IT OFF

The organs of the press
Record he lies
There, beautifully expressionless,
On the white and holey sheets:
Spent trying archaic dying,
Come too (through), drying,
Dead to the whirl,
Headed no more,
Simply there-there
In the honey mood.

NEAR-OCCASIONAL POEM

Ask me a question. Tell me a lie.
Come, or hum, or hit me.
Send me away; send it away.
Drink, or sleep, or let me feel your ignoring.
Hold my hand when you scold me.
At least scold—whom you no longer hold.
Seem busy; play with yourself.
Open magic boxes. Drown for the good of our soul.

HOKKU

the ice splits a man
wakes dying a child falls
to sleep now in church.

HOKKU

The sun: a warm hand
Touching my chest now—with light
And loving sunstrokes.

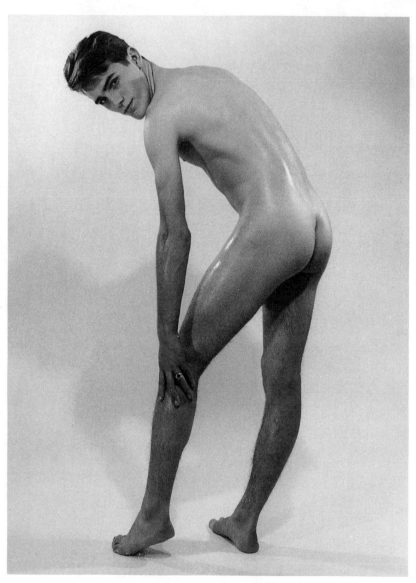

Bill Rice photographed by Troy Saxon

ON B. R. 1

    Damn it all though—
        I love you, you Yo-Yo.
Look how I know, though:
        You're big there—and aware.
Photographically pure, true-blue, you—
        I lust after, lap up—grow on me, you know.
From teen-age gravure, you woo, you
        Reach out your hairy dare,
Your transcendental velvet, soapstone hide unhid;
        Thoughtless, heedless—doubtless, undid:
You stand there, your bare back to me;
        You want that I want you not just here to see. Be.

You powdered-sugar-honey bee sting me
        As you glow your deepset glower power yet,
Looking nude, back, and rightout;
        Rude stanchion of a witless soul duet.
Black hair, black brows, and blackeyes on grout
        Sing a streakless mesmerizing pout.

    Your spheres turn this music to a voice in rejoice.
        The vulgar muscles begin to lose
Taut and cheeky dimples in muse-box fiction
        As organgrinding Allboy orders still issues
In a weak and studied nasal diction,
        With limp and toying dental lisp ruse.

You hum me "I love you" with all of my might
        And imprint with the looking the rites of this plight—
As salamander eyewhites hypnotize with sanpaku;
        And the man, the child, and the boy are two.

ROADSIDE STAND

A hitchhiker ass-hauls along the highway, on the right.
My truck jerks for a pickup, so, in the night.
He gives me a leg up and in.
I give him a meal. I feel: he's so thin-within.

He goggles at, goes for
The reststop classical floozy
who antedates the hustling that I serve.
I encourage him to drive then
his (he thinks) somethingbetter bargain.

Thumbing, he did take a chance-and get it.
She may smell of pay in advance-and yet it
's true after they do whatever they do,

>   She'll go home alone,
>   But he'll have one to go to.

BOY

Box of sweets, compacted lay,
Your skimpy-sideburned youth
Suggests a slick and hairless chest
And restive late pubescence.
Your Greek and little nose
Reveals your restless organ grows
No more than those
Exquisite parts of ancient Greeks
Remembered in their arts.

A MAN: A SORT OF SESTINA

Heaven sent man you boy
with overdeveloped deltoi-
ds and the perfect flaw of nothing to spoi-
l the noi-
seless gobs of beauty that overjoy
us all at a ducky decoy.

Nothing spoi-
ls the unconscious, sleepy, tearstained languor you encoin,
bustling by boi-
sterously. Toi-
ling with your tool, you know not you enjoy
us to annoy.

That we may rejoi-
ce in the glorious noi-
se uncoi-
ling from the up-hautboy-
s-and-away within-you earthless pretuned unsoiled spoi-
l, play on your food-of-love little toy.

Noi-
some, coy
playboy—
oh! no! why, why are you putting it away? You toy
with us only to the meaty meanness point. Killjoy.

Invent prudery, Prudence; tidy your toi-
let; recoi-
l noi-
sily and, yes, even poi-

gnantly. We still in with you joi-
n. You still all the more buoy.
Coi-
ling within, you despoi-
l within God's house. Yet let us you annoi-
nt that from your conscience toi-
l you may somesoonday forthflower, alterboy,
godkin of joy.

A man.

SENRYU

His red-leather lips
Open (my wallet) into
A white fecal street.

OH, TO KEEP BEAUTY BACK FROM VANISHING AWAY

Your face is beautiful,
Indescribably beautiful as I pass by,
Beautiful and beautiful and beautiful:
And more beautiful still.

Then as I pass completely around you,
I see that you dare to go further.
And I am drooling
Over the exquisite and imagined dueling

That went into your two parallel
Your too perfect,
Cheeky
Scars.

BARSTOP

Hot light hanging over him across the bar and into the goods.
Out of the side of your oh so oh boy mouth.
Out of the snide of her oh so oi icicle hot hardness.
Cover your face in sorrow.
Ply her jewish shrewishness.
Play your man thing, boy.
Across the noise and into the coulds.
Across the boys and into.
Fake it well.
Play the heavy.
Slay the bevy.
Lay the red-headed dragon.
(Pound louder, music; grow longer, sideburns.)
The levantine sings,
Louder.
She swings.
She slings it.
Around, the very boy comes, impressing his teeshirt.
Wicked which of the north suck-hums.
So they all say.
But so they do.

STRAIGHT

He's so perfect
As he sits on the edge of his chair
There,
His back so straight,
His legs parted so.
He's so straight:
Greeknosed, straightnosed.
He rises.
He stands straight,
Ægean-posed, the
Talked-to
Center
Of everyone attentions.
He walks straight ahead,
Straight away.
He's straight enough
To wear,
Unaware,
An expansion band.
Yes, he
Would be
Wearing
A wedding
Thing.

HOKKU

April snow flurries.
Down-settling on the bed.
After a pillow fight.

PAUL CALL

I never did want to be like you, your mere friend.
    I like/liked you to be near.
I need you to play with because anymore you don't like me.
    I am your offensive offense.
You are my All-American near-miss, flower-crushing bruiser.
    But I'm your penance.
Dear man with the super man-thing,
    a superboy body, you dear queer,

Get up and come, come get it,
    make a pass, run, touch
Down. Pillow-prop; play ball, Paul; maul me.
    Charge and tackle and foul and overstep the line, mine.
Lie down. Feel goal.
    Rollagain over. Autograph-sign.
Open your swell-dimpled hips, lips.
    Give me your nevermore nonelike nonesuch somuch.

You knead an opposite to hole together.
    The acid high in your Gatorading trough
Has to be a me. But
    I can't I now know be that
Me for you because
    you see I see/like you through a tooreal-ly unreal lens.

All right already, go.
    How can you like me afterall after I want you, mere mesomorph?
I know I couldn't-
    and can't respect the man who'd settle-down me, for or with. Drat.
Really roll over; beteammate your friends. Anything with a beginning
    agains, but everything in the end rearends.

SOME CHILDREN

Shutting her other out to in your own,
Proving her other self your home and own,

You touch your nose;
You hold her chin,
Grit your teeth, ungrin,
Guard your guardian chesthouse,
Dwell in your manjacketing temple of fur.

You know the bird knows she talktalks unlistened.
You smother nymphhood,
Sibyl silence.
Castlekeep,
Play your queen.

SOME CHILDREN

Student lover, looking kisses,
You show us our childhood. Your matted
Hairs lie quiet; hers glisten.
You will be her lap-robe:
With wristback gentletouch
You slowdraw her head unto yours.
You luxuriate in the adulthood of it all, and she
Drinks myopia from your unglassed boyface.   Then
You will
    not to want her, brokenglass. You
Wet roselip slips, chew gum, blow
Smokescreens, think love at her, and
Love, and so give
Up. Glossy face affirms new desire;
New man comes through, winning
The hard way. Happy boy,
Could we only keep you up forever—
Could we only keep you up for now.

EPISTLE TO THE MOD CHURCH

Dear Rock, I love you.
Peter, Peter, peter-eater,
Thou art Pierre;
And upon this derrière,
With stone gall in my hard,
I raise my movie house to you.

PASSING

I
Eleven heads rim
The huddling sphincter. Clap.
Break, play unfolding.

II
The footballing boys
Grown away—now the mourning
Of the dry, cracked mud.

TRACK MEAT

Don and Jeff are beautiful a-
track.
The beautiful people always get to
know each other,
get to no all others.
Their attraction is tight and hard and daring.

Bronze by indigo made the hoofirons merely ring.
You give each other a run
for the ring;
you ring each other.
With this ring you
will out in the end.

Bodyboybeautifuls, you have the ends
to end all ends.
You, Bronze, with the turned up knows back there,
end your lonely nightstreet alwayswandering
through him, with him, in him.
Drink him in.

Indigo Eyesaskew,
you with your perfect flaw,
draw him to.
Some tomorrow rue the raw.
Tonight,
light.

Lift his little apples lightly, hardbody you
whoever.
Die green world—in their fun.
Cloverover. Peg in. Done.

Begin
again. Tat for tit, sharealiking.

You
love
love.
It
loves
you.

You love.
Love it.
Love you.

HOKKU

My lover's gentle
Snore—a fly buzz in the night.
He won't go away.

SENRYU

do i love you
because you re beautiful
are you

OLD JERSEY

O elegant off-duty eating-out jock
With your dripping football jersey hanging
    out and all over,
I see you before me paired off for dinner,
    and everything's just
About right about you: the bangs
    to the brows,
The beard coming in, the skin
As white as the creamy insides of things,
    the sugar lump
Of a chin, and the chest that's too big—
    with its
(This most of all) casual jersey still bigger.
    You
Show you coolly know how to control
    the, broad
Qualities there are in you with that new
Tear there at the shoulder of the sliding
And shining and beautifully used
    return-again-to
Old jersey.
When you get up, pick check up, you
Smile and stuff foldfuls necessary
    of the front
Of that jersey
Into incredibly fitting, quite bleachy jeans.
    So,
A floating surface of
    jersey moves from the shoulders.
And with ball-bearing bearing smiling hips
    swing round so slick
Inside old jersey:

Though you may not show
Basket, you certainly know
How to haul ass. As you jab at the jersey
    with smart forky hands,
Shifted and shuffling, you've launched
    all that limberness
The sailor's at sea—before she
Can possibly know where you
    want her to go, O
Perfectly pretty behindhand,
Clearly aboveboard boy.

FRATERNITY

Hey you, Animal!
Vegetable?
Protein?
Fish!
Well, hell I can wish,
Can't I?

FRATERNITY

Why don't you be like your
Brother,
Worldlywise,
Workmanlike,
Butch, and
Sporty?

BELOW THE BELT

This is the joy
   Of the fraternity boy,
This is the trick
   Of being slick—
Look over the world
   As prospects for pledging, as if
They were the mere cattle one's
   Womanly chattel are—
In one's dry reality,
   Not dreams.

ANOTHER ANNIVERSARY

He's so hard,
        and hee's so soft.
He's so butch,
        and hee's so pretty.
He's so commanding,
        and hee's so agreeable.
He's so eagleeyed and blind;
        hee's so sane and silly.
He's so loose and lumbering;
        hee's so tight and exact.
He's so sugary-and-caky;
        hee's so tart and bittersweet.
They're so opposite
        and together.
He keeps His legs apart.
        hee enjambs hiss thighs. But the
        apartment of hiss legs
is enjambment, the old moist, with sighs.

HOKKU

Your bark is broken,
Rough, and old—but your every
Leaf's a valentine.

SENRYU

He retracts
The foreskin of the stormy sky—
I see the moon.

CATCH

The garters remain perfect and tight,
And the aluminum buttonworks works.
The rest is dishevelment,
Prettily dirty
And faded
And sweaty and torn.
The cheeks of the ass come home to grass
On this first pretty baseballer
I ever saw.
But his uniform comes to seem dandy
Because he is. It's
His refinelined face and delicate features
Give grace to his
After-a-hard-day-o'play,
Doggy
Exhaustion.

NO ACCIDENT

As our truck passes alongside his, I
Look at him, and
He looks at me,
And we see
Each other.

Above the cab of his truck
In cursive letters—
"Miss Linda."

But which is the miss,
The other truck
Or the other trucker?

SEEN

His mother-fucker of purl-one face knits to cheese-cloth rating guarding grinding cheekbone ivory carving.
 "Ruinous, runny confection-dodger, you sargasso-sea me, mirrorback, stare for stare, you with your blue-hair dare."
 His narrow gorge of hipping, dipping dripping thighs unfar ajar, beats on and off inthrough the mind into the mouth a leg-bowed promised land.
 "Frugal, fugal bugle rex, googolplex sexhex, as my boat-soul goat-hole goes swifting in the rifting strands of rhyme, do you know which hand your meat is buttered on?"

SEEN

Your swaggering cigar
Caught by the tail
In the vice of your incisors,
The cream in your eyes,
The oil-slick film of the suntan
Over your rocky face
Protect you from the world,
From the traces
Of worldliness in you,
Who merely do
But don't like to admit
It. You swagger so swishly.

PLAY BY EAR

I like to look at you, Look Away,
Scrumptious scroungy sunbleached sideburns,
Hardboiled lips, and beaded eyes and all.
I need to look, through you, to you.
   I like the taste of you, Won't Do,
   When you shoot into white clouds,
   Then root down to earth, awaiting rebirth.
   I need to do self-sufficient you.

   Unmoved, you dance in my mind and
   Prance on my every little kindness. But
   I need your beauty to feed me (are we through?),
Need your pretense of a freed you.
And I want you to need me-and like you to.
And I do (it's true), I too, need you.

A PHI DELT IN CHARBERT'S: A SONNET ON IT

   There is nothing Greek about you⁻
Unless perhaps your curls in swirls
(Yellowing with lack of age and the care of cares),
Or the stencil on your not-a-letter sweater,
Or your hellenistically no-ing, knowing
Dark cavernous eyecaverns, urns.
No, there's nothing greek about sleek you:
The gold on top, the darkling darker brows,
The azure in the blank reflecting depths (you seek you)⁻
We've seen and drunk all your before, before.

   Oh. Though: your bold and square black-and-silver pinkyfingering ring.
   Behind then: your overall allover pink-tan tan.
   And your greekgodlike⁻goddamn you⁻beauty, Beauty.
And your unbeatable, unconceitable conceit⁻you know, you know.

EDMUND MILLER ♂♂

HOKKU

Ripening plums
Heave bosoms in the wind—
Almost bloodready.

HOKKU

Pretty red flowers,
Are you weighted with dew now
From reaming the night?

TWO SIDES

I
"You're so smooth."
"You should'a' been a girl."
"Boy, you have pretty eyes."

My three praises
So far. But then
I've only known him five months.

II
Look at your hairy shadow on the wall!
Oh, don't turn over!
My, how hard your dimples are back here!
Oh, stop that! You're turning me on.

Five seconds.

ACCUMULATED INTEREST

I
Your classical hawking indian roman nose.
Your dead delirious now forefront scar.
Your romantic snowflake deciduous dandruff.
Your beating incomplete wrong head.
Your braggart wideangle gait.
Your naked asphalt interior.
   Unbelievable, exciting, ugly.

II
Your straight quiet simmering peachy nose.
Your grassy wintergreen my-lady-of-the-night eyes.
Your thirsting whispered hair.
Your curly off-light almost-white head.
Your listing footfall began.
Your sticky elastic glass creamboat.
   Daring, plain, mere beauty.

HOKKU

The horny moon
Vades in the predawn sky–
The rising sun.

HOKKU

Off the Dover coast:
The world around us all fog—
Now black-breasted rocks.

INCIDENT

inquisitive straightacross eyebrows
crumpled into dark questions.
questing, stucktogether eyelash eyeshades
over cro-magnon tarpits of midnight browning.
beautifully rebellious and almost white teeth.

swollen, marooned lips.
darkling cheeks of undisguisable, sprouting
manhair—why i

haven't even done the head
yet, and the devil's gone and
come already.

INCIDENT

As I try to remember
Whether children dream,
You turn over in my sleep and say,
"Try it again."

But then when I try it again,
You touch me just when.
You chew it again:
"Do you remember when . . . ?"

"You're out of your mind."
Fucking shit. At it again?
"Stop it! Damn it!
This shit fucks with my mind."

You just did it again.
"But we used to have fun—
What ever became of your fucking technique?"
Well . . . , you didn't need it then.

HOKKU

Stunning cold autumn—
Bluejays all over the lawn,
Nuts in their beaks.

HOKKU

Half-naked, quite
Pink, and fall-befallen—
The maple tree.

SUCKING UP

O Loyal Fan FiGi Steve, inevitably you cock
Your eye at the passing ass of that jock.

You check out the buttock swishing (you soar)
Of any overstuffed and available whore.

But now then, careening beyond the edge
Of all decent and masculine carriage,

The heavy humps before you muscle-pull
Up short. An assy hunk fleshy, full-

Bottomed, hulking (your heart leaping) stops,
Puts hand to hip. Your mouth drops.

Before you, for you, the knightless ship
Hellos. And you feel his hello hand touch your hip.

Stigmata'd, blinded, later you say,
"What, . . . what a man I saw today!"

QUICKIE

Wow!
   You too?
And how!
Right now?

   Screw?
Who?
   You.
Hell, no!

   Well, blow?
Again who?
   Again you.

Two way, please?
   Go blow, tease.

SEEN

Big and happy, you're no hippie.
Curly hair is not enough.
A cleft chin doesn't lie.
Your bones are smooth;
Your sweater's vee'd.
The suntan makes makebelieve your scene.
Though romansandaled, you're manhandled.

THE DAYDREAM OF A PROFESSIONAL IN SIXTEENTH-CENTURY PROSE AND ELIZABETHAN DRAMA EXCLUDING SHAKESPEARE— AND IN BUT LITTLE ELSE

Beautiful scholar,
Ascham's Euphues,
Pensive in a cloister alcove,
Pencil between your bare toes,
Prehensile to my Udall touch,
Holy Innocent as you buy it—
And I buy that.

SENRYU

I swing:
My cuntland—it's with thee,
Inexplicably.

INDEX OF FORMS

Epigrams: 2, 41, 42, 47
Grooks: 2, 24, 37, 45, 47, 66
Haiku poetry: 5, 8, 16, 17, 24, 28, 33, 36, 37, 44, 45, 52, 53, 56, 57, 60, 61, 66
Sestinas: 22, 34
Sonnets: 6, 9, 19, 20, 29, 50, 51, 62, 63

ALLUSION INDEX

Arnold, Matthew 57
Ascham, Roger 65
Bara, Theda 12
Bashō 5, 8, 16, 17, 28, 33, 36, 44, 52, 53, 56, 57, 60, 61
Dickinson, Emily 36
Donne, John 6, 43
Edward VII 4
Eliot, T[homas] S[terns] 12
Euripides 2
Frost, Robert 6, 62
Goldsmith, Oliver 12
Green, Robert 12
Gunn, Thom 6, 62
Hart, William S. 12
Hein, Piet 2, 24, 37, 45, 47, 66
Herbert, George 21, 42
Hopkins, Gerard Manley 29
Hudson, Rock 32
Joyce, James 34, 48
Kafka, Franz 12
Keats, John 8
Key, Francis Scott 66
Lyly, John 65
Peele, George 12
Pound, Ezra 22, 34
Shakespeare, William 2, 65
Shelley, Percy Bysshe 13
Sidgwick, Frank 63
Tchaikovsky, Pëtr Ilych 12
Udall, Nicholas 65
Williams, William Carlos 52

A MORE SPORTING INDEX

Baseball: 46
Bodybuilding: 22-23
Chess: 30
Dueling: 25
Fencing: 25
Football: 7, 29, 33, 38, 62
Hockey: 11
Ice hockey: 11
Lacrosse: 6
Modeling: 19
Movie work: 12, 32
Pillow fights: 28
Pledging: 40, 41, 42, 51, 62
Running: 34-35
Sunbathing: 17, 49, 50, 51
Track: 34-35
Trade: 20, 24, 50, 58
Truck driving: 20, 47
Weight training: 22-23
Whacking off: 1-66

WORDS NOT KNOWN TO THE WORDPERFECT™ SPELLCHECK

Arcana æolian, anagrammatic, callipygian, donnée, hautboy, quadriviality, sanpaku
Contractions asks'm, o'play, should'a', wanderlusting's, y'r
Fragmentary words annoi-, boi-, -ce, coi-, deltoi-, despoi-, -ds, -gnantly, joi-, -ls, noi-, -nt, recoi-, rejoi-, -seless, -sily, spoi-, -sterously, toi-, uncoi-
French à, crosse, derrière, donnée, levantine, oi
Inflections agains, anagrammatic, assy, baseballer, beteammate, bleachy, catamites, coulds, earthless, enjambs, eyelining, foldfuls, footballing, forky, Gatorading, godkin, happied, hellenistically, hipping, -ing, knightless, -ly, manjacketing, -ness, nighthood, nymphhood, organgrinding, pinkyfingering, pretuned, quadriviality, questing, rearends, refinelined, rinky, romansandaled, scroungy, shakealiking, sodomize, stigmata'd, streakless, sunbleached, swifting, swishly, tonguing, Twentyish, unconceitable, undisguisable, unfar, unglassed, ungrin, unhid, unlistened, vee'd, wanderlusting, welling, womby
Miscellaneous bluejays, cloze, drat, encoin, goddamn, googolplex, hardbody, hautboy, -ing, levantine, -ly, makebelieve, -ness, oi, quadriviality, rinky, sargasso, shit
Poetic coinages alterboy, cloze, encoin, godkin, hee, unhid
Proper names Ægean, æolian, Allboy, Ascham, Charbert's, Chris, Cro-Magnon, Delt, Donne, Euphues, Eyesaskew, FiGi, Gatorading, Greene, hellenistically, Jeff, Udall, Wakefield
Run-together words afterall, Allboy, allover, alterboy, alwayswandering, barstop, blackeyes, bloodready, bluejays, bodyboybeautifuls, boychicks, boyface, brokenglass, buttonworks, castlekeep, chesthouse, cloverover, creamboat, cuntland, deepset, eagleeyed, eyecaverns, eyelining, Eyesaskew, eyeshadow, eyewhites, forthflower, gentletouch, glassdoor, goddamn, greekgodlike, Greeknosed, hardbody, hardboiled, headfilling, headsize, hoofirons, inthrough, lockerroom, makebelieve, manhair, manjacketing, mirrorback, nighthood, nightstreet, nonelike, organgrinding, pinkyfingering, realitynight, rearends, refinelined, reststop, rightout, rollagain, romansandled, roselip, sexhex, shakealiking, sideburned, slowdraw, smokescreens, somesoonday, somethingbetter, somuch, straightacross, strightnosed, stucktogether, sunbleached, superboy, takeback, talktalks, tarpits, teeshirt, tooreal, underjersey, wanderlusting, wideangle, worldywise, wristback

Sex words callipygian, cuntland, derrière, fucker, fucking, fucks, rearends, sodomize
Technical terms callipygian, enjambs, Euphues, googolplex, hokku, sanpaku, sargasso, senryu, sestina

AFTERWORD

SUGAR KANE
"You know, I'm gonna be twenty-five in June."

JOE AS JOSEPHINE
"You are?"

SUGAR KANE
"That's a quarter of a century. Makes a girl think."

JOE AS JOSEPHINE
"About what?"

—Billy Wilder and I. A. L. Diamond, *Some Like It Hot*

Since what was originally a privately published book has been selling steadily now for twenty years unadvertized and unavailable in bookstores, I am hoping it might find a broader audience in the present climate of greater acceptance of gay publications. Although the original edition was typeset at The Poet's Press, the book design was my own, including the cover with the title showing through on the back in mirror writing and the page logo of two overlapping male symbols (I could not get this to come out quite so nicely now that I do my own typesetting on the computer).

For the most part, the poems in *Fucking Animals* were written and put into final form in the late sixties while I was a graduate student at Ohio State. I suppose I was learning to be a poet and learning to be gay at the same time, and the conjunction had interesting implications for this volume. There is an experimental wildness to the verse here and also perhaps to the life experiences evoked. I would not be the writer I am now if I had not gone through this period, nor would I be the person I am now.

Apart from adding this Afterword and two new indexes and changing the art and layout, the revisions for this edition I have kept to a minimum. Had I attempted to revise extensively, the youthful wildness might have vanished in the mists like Brigadoon. What I have done, apart from correcting a few typographical errors, is rectify the lineation of "Track Meat" and the attendant problems in poem order. "Track Meat" as it stands in this edition is now more like the very imperfect sestina it was always intended to be. The incomplete imperfection of that poem in the volume as originally published left it so short that it fit on one page, throwing off the facing page patterns of all the subsequent poems. While the book was in press in 1973 I moved around a few poems to correct some of the havoc I saw. But I can no longer locate the original order, and in trying to right things to show the original parallels, I have found myself rearranging things quite a bit. I hope that the new ordering will reveal unexpected connections. I have a feeling that "On B. R. 1" and "Paul Call" were intended at one time to be on facing pages since each is a sonnet in sprung rhythm making a fanciful reading of the romantic other. The extremely full half-lines being quite overwhelming in each poem by itself, it is now clear to me that they should be kept separated like hyperactive children. The internal rhymes in these poems and another pair of separated sonnets, "Eyeful" and "A Phi Delt in Charbert's," are part of their Hopkinsesque legacy.

Gerard Manley Hopkins is, in fact, an influence much in evidence throughout the book. Among other such pervasive influences is George Herbert, about whom I have written extensively in a number of scholarly books. Herbert is undoubtedly the source of the pattern of title repetition, and there is a specific allusion to his poem "Vertue" in "Boy." John Donne may be responsible for some of the enjambment in "Donnée," which alludes to him in a number of ways, although I cannot think he would look kindly on a pattern of irregular couplets. The oxymoronic idea of writing a sonnet in couplets (as also "Sucking Up") may show the influence of Robert Frost-or is it Thom Gunn? The short lines of the sonnet "Quickie" I distinctly remember working out under the inspiration of "Aeronaut to His Lady" by Frank Sidgwick. The arcane images and general tone of "Pæderastia" clearly owe something to T. S. Eliot and perhaps to Ezra Pound. In reviewing my files, I discovered an elaborate set of footnotes I once thought it worthwhile to compose for "Pæderastia," supposing it might be necessary not only to supply definitions of everything from "drag" to "polymorphous perverse" but also to explain that Madras was a fashionable preppie plaid and that silent film star Theda Bara was so peculiar looking that she was rumored to be a man in said drag. I did discover among these notes two points I had forgotten that might be useful to preserve for posterity: the trendy sixties discothèque Arthur had an official policy of not admitting unescorted males, and Catholic Charities did at one time actually use the slogan "Tender, caring psychiatry."

"The Daydream" also makes some arcane literary allusions. Euphues, which is the Greek for "good-looking guy," is the hero of an interminable prose romance in precious style by John Lyly. Roger Ascham and Nicholas Udall were famous sixteenth-century schoolmasters. Udall got into some little trouble for having sex with his students, although perhaps not so much trouble as many people think he should have.

The haiku poetry shows a reading of Bashô and other Japanese masters, but placing these poems in the context of this book has the effect of making them more personal and more erotic than they must have appeared to the editors who unsuspectingly printed them in haiku magazines. That is why I used the term "hokku"—to distance these poems to some extent from the Japanese tradition. In this tradition, senryu are personal evocations in haiku form, but mine are pretty much over the top of tradition. I might have called them grooks after Piet Hein, if I had been familiar with his work at the time. However, although very untraditional in their erotic imagery, all the hokku and senryu here are formally within the haiku tradition. Anyone who still thinks that somehow syllable counting can have any evocative power in English should look at Harold Henderson's wonderful little study *Haiku in English*.

I had not originally thought to comment on the reviews of the first edition in this Afterword, but culling them for promotional quotations at the suggestion of my publisher, I was surprised to discover how beside the point they all were, even in their praise. No reviewer so much as mentioned the experimentation with the sonnet before the fashionable revival of that form. The elaborate wordplay and intricate patterns of internal rhyme were passed over in silence by Jim Eggeling in *The Advocate*, although he should have been the perfect reviewer to notice them precisely because these elements characterize his own poetry. It cannot even be said that reviewers focused on the content in deference to the likely audience since they fixated curiously on the four-line poem "Women," the first after the prologue poem "Parking." Michael Perkins in *Screw* thought "Women" quite the best poem in the volume. Eggeling, however, thought this poem epitomized all that was worst about the volume because of its blatant anti-feminism. While raising an objection that is surely as perverse as faulting *Pride and Prejudice* for the shallowness of its commentary on the Napoleonic Wars, he noticed in the poem neither the allusion to the "greasy Joan" of the song that concludes *Love's Labour's Lost* nor the allusion to the phantom Helen of the play by Euripides. He gave no indication of noticing the condom joke. He also missed the celebration of cuntland in the parallel framing poem at the end of the book. At any rate, the attitude toward women that characterizes these poems is jealousy of their hold over men, not rejection. And if there is an emotional limitation here it is voyeurism, not misogyny. I can only hope that the next round of reviewers will be more astute.

General readers will probably be interested in the personal as well as the literary antecedents of these poems. The material is grounded in real experience, but most of the experience was vicarious. There is a hot number behind almost every poem but not usually a hot date. I was discovering sex at the time, but unrequited longings rather than actual encounters seemed to drive my poetic inspiration. The dedication to the 1969 Ohio State football team is, for example, pure cheek: since I received my M.A. and left the school that year, the inspiring team was really the 1968 one (it did play in the Rose Bowl on New Year's Day in 1969). Although the guys who inspired most of these poems were not personally known to me, I did try to find out their names, and I still have this information in a file with the foul papers and early drafts of the poems. While it is too soon to be revealing such information, literary executors please take note.

"Edwardian Insight" and "The Daydream" were actually written at Duke, where I spent a semester before moving on to Ohio State. There is at Duke a study room with alcoves that is very conducive to intense concentration of various sorts, and these two poems were originally composed on the spot. I cannot reconstruct the name of either guy, but I have to suppose that one of them was named Edward.

Moving on to Ohio State, I note that "Donnée" is about a lacrosse player named Greg, although the point is fairly obvious in the poem. He had a strange and beautiful surname, which I must yet keep from the world. I never so much as spoke to him, but his beauty haunts me still to this day. The hockey goalie commemorated in "Most Valuable Rookie" I think I never even saw in person, but his picture in the Ohio State *Lantern* was inspiration enough. In that photograph he is caught with his mouth agape and yet in the throes of happiness. I do not know whether the picture was taken when he learned of the award or at a game (it cannot have been during play because he is not wearing his mask). I still have a copy of the picture.

"On B. R. 1" commemorates another photographic inspiration. It is about a model named Bill Rice. B. R. 1 is the code for a set of photographs of him from the Troy Saxon Gallery. Since this was a long time ago, none of the pictures are frontal nudes, although there is one at an odd angle where you can by accident actually see everything. Lean and pretty (usually not my type), Bill Rice had remarkable inviting eyes, as commemorated in the poem. An examination of the photographs with the clearer vision of today reveals no evidence, however, that he had sanpaku, the magical condition in which the whites show below the iris. He was monstrously well hung, as can be seen in the evidence of various bulges and the one peekaboo frontal exposure in that same photographic record. But it was the eyes, I am sure: I have always been a sucker for eyelashes.

"Paul Call," the other sprung-rhythm sonnet, is about someone who was a walk-on freshman football player at Ohio State my first year there. Whenever I saw him about campus, he was always paired up with another fellow, someone with the same top-heavy halfback body but without Paul's milk-fed good looks. I remember hearing a story about the two of them involving the Phi Delta Theta Fraternity and a request their pledge class made of the fraternity pimp (I know this sounds highly improbable as I write it, and I cannot vouch for the story's accuracy but am only repeating what I heard at the time); what they requested was a boy. The implication is that women were brought in on a more regular basis. Those availing themselves of the special service on this occasion did so two by two (perhaps this was a hazing exercise to bond them in shared illicit activity), and of course Paul and his friend made up one of the pairs. The friend wanted to get rimmed, but the boy would not comply. My source for this story is the boy, who reported that the friend settled for a blow job while Paul fucked him (grammatically that "him" is ambiguous, but I think I shall leave it). I do not think that either Paul or his friend ever made it into professional football.

"Two Sides" is one of the few poems that records an actual sexual encounter. The guy had a surname right out of a handyman's toolbox. As the poem indicates, the fellow's obdurate taciturnity was one of his principal charms. Actually, he never said anything much at all unless he was on acid. He preferred to have sex that way too. I think perhaps he enjoyed the idea of sex with a teacher (a mere graduate assistant) more than the actual mansex. One Sunday afternoon we had sex in my office on the eighth floor of Denney Hall: we could see out across campus for quite a distance. I was helped a lot in the speed and enthusiasm with which I made the final revisions on my master's thesis by a drug he gave me that is now called ecstasy.

The Don and Jeff of "Track Meat" were two cool beauties of different types, as the poem indicates. I knew Jeff slightly. It was Don, however, who became an obsession despite the fact that I never met him. Don was the blond. I had seen each of the two many times previously under a variety of circumstances. The poem was inspired by seeing them together for the first time one day on the street. It was a Friday afternoon, and they were not doing anything in particular, just walking together, aimlessly talking about what they might do that night-so far as I could overhear. It was just their being together that somehow put them definitively out of my reach in a way that I had not noticed before. There is one story about Don by himself that sticks in my memory with special clarity. It was another weekend, but this time it was late at night. When I first spotted him he was talking to a black kid, I mean a child, a six- or seven-year-old. I could not hear what was being said from my vantage point, but it was all very much out in the open, and I imagined that the kid was lost and that Don was just being helpful, perhaps agreeing to call the kid's parents. As they moved off hand in hand, I followed along—at a discreet distance of course—more because I always enjoyed watching Don than for any other reason. But the odd couple attracted the attention of a pair of football player types who, judging from their body language, were putting a very different interpretation on things than I was. Don turned up Fraternity Row (really Fifteenth Avenue), a broad, well-lighted street, and the caravan of interested others went right along. When Don suddenly turned and climbed the steps up to one of the fraternity houses, the two football types rushed ahead, obviously worried that they might lose track of the action. But I just happened to know where Don was living at the time, and this was in the next street. He had obviously taken Fraternity Row for the lighting. I too climbed a set of steps, but I did not have to run ahead to take the same set he was using since I knew where he was going. From my place in the shadows of the alley, I chaperoned Don safely home with the boy and then watched as the other two rushed about in confusion unable to figure out how he had vanished. Then I went home, quite pleased with Don and probably not a little with myself too.

A "Phi Delt in Charbert's" commemorates two of the most distinctive institutions of Ohio State in the sixties. Charbert's was an all-night restaurant just across High St. from the main entrance to the University. During the day it was relatively neutral territory, patronized by all sorts, but of course at night the only people there tended to be night people—druggies, street people, gays. I actually made my first sexual pick up there. I had been to gay bars quite a few times and had acquired a number of gay friends, but it is hard to get sex going the first time. At any rate, I found it a lot easier after I had gotten started with that first guy in Charbert's. But this poem is not about that incident. It is really not about an incident at all. It is just mostly about the anomaly of seeing a Phi Delt in Charbert's late at night. I probably would have marked the guy down as a likely Phi Delt even without the letters ΦΔΘ emblazoned across his chest. Phi Delta Theta, although I neglected to point the fact out when I mentioned that house of wet dreams in another context, was the beauty house. The brothers all had pretty faces and broad shoulders. And they all seemed to possess a negative capability of cool self-possession that I found almost more exciting than their good looks. Their huge fraternity house was conveniently located next to the Newman Center, and interestingly enough both rather than Hopkins sounds the keynote of this other collection. The poems in the collection are again evocations of youthful exuberance reconstructed by the outsider. While not explicitly gay, they are homoerotic in the sense that each is a portrait of a guy pictured in a moment when he is doing something most characteristic, often showing off.

And my gay erotic fiction has also accumulated to the point where I am looking for a publisher for *Nighttimes*. These stories have appeared in *Blueboy*, *Honcho*, and *Playguy* and in several anthologies edited by John Patrick, for example *Huge*, *Seduced*, and *Big Boys/Little Lies*. Most of these are still available from STARBooks (PO Box 2737, Sarasota FL 34230-2737). My long nostalgic story "Game Nights" in Patrick's *Runaways/Kid Stuff* compensates, I hope, for the absence of a basketball poem in *Fucking Animals*. For a critical study of gay erotic literature in general, I refer readers to the article I wrote on "Erotica and Pornography" for *Gay and Lesbian Literary Heritage*, edited by Claude J. Summers (New York: Henry Holt, 1995). As I have written gay fiction in later years, I have discovered myself able to make greater use of real experience than I did in the early poetry. In the novel *Two Sisters* the character Gore Vidal comments to the character who obviously represents Anaïs Nin that she invents nothing, at which point she counterclaims that he himself (and by implication Gore Vidal the author of that book) makes everything up. I must be more of a Vidal in poetry and a Nin in fiction, although in fiction as in life the sex sometimes has to be embellished to make it last. But in the end it comes to pretty much the same thing, whether one is writing about the experiences one has or about those one does not.

♂♂

Thanks to John Q. Sillari for sharp-eyed help with proofreading.

Cover design by John Patrick.

Photographs of Bill Rice by Troy Saxon reproduced courtesy of Dream Maker Productions, 1626 N. Wilcox Ave Suite 488, Los Angeles CA 90028.

Caricature of the author by himself.

About the Author

Edmund Miller is Professor of English and Department Chairman at the C. W. Post Campus of Long Island University. In addition to poetry in little magazines, he is the author of several other books of poetry, including most recently *The Happiness Cure*. His erotic stories have appeared in *Honcho*, *Mandate*, *Playguy*, *Blueboy*, and numerous anthologies. He is also the author of scholarly books about seventeenth-century British literature, most recently a genealogy of George Herbert.